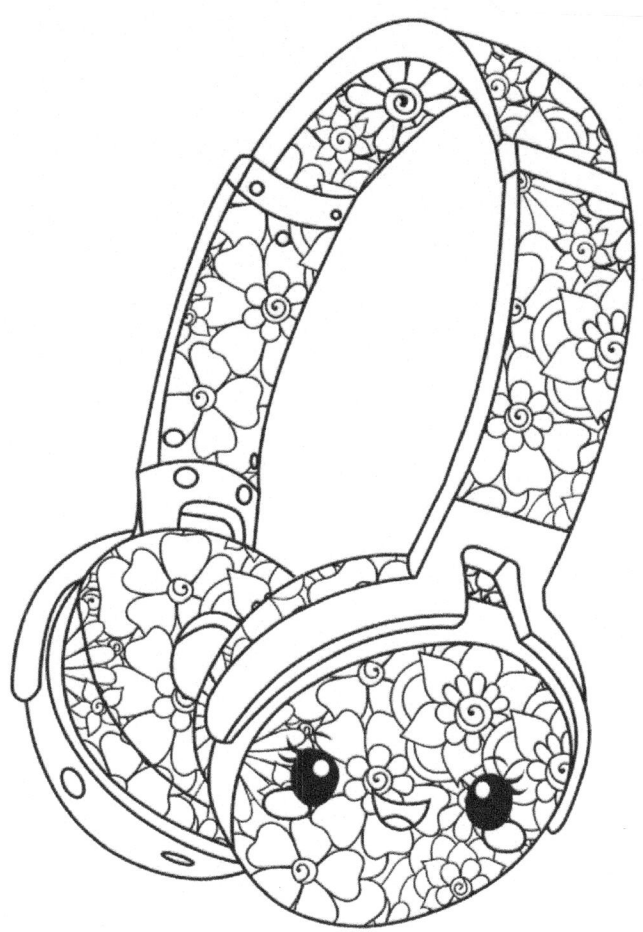

This Book Belongs To:

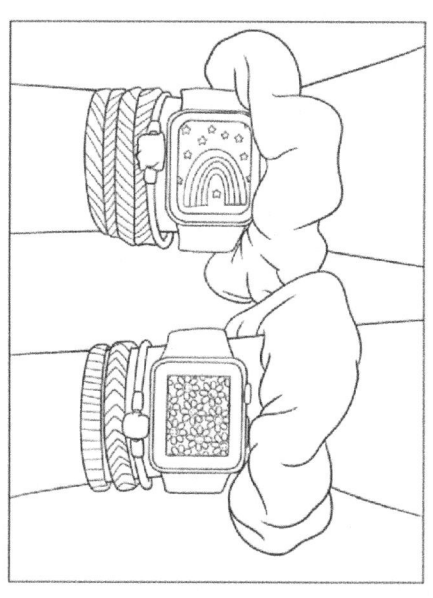

Thank you for your purchase!

We are a small, family run business and appreciate each and every order...

Want some FREE printable coloring pages?

For your FREE printable coloring pages, please join our mailing list at:

www.ellastevensondesigns.com

or

◎ @ellastevensondesigns

© Copyright 2022 - All rights reserved by EllaStevensonDesigns

Legal notice. This book is only for personal use. The contents of the book may not be reproduced, duplicated or transmitted without direct written permission from the author, except small sections for review purposes.

Color Test Page

A quick tip:
The paper Amazon uses to print coloring books is best suited for colored pencils and gel pens. If using felt tip pens, we recommend putting a piece of card or paper behind the page you are coloring to prevent any bleed through.

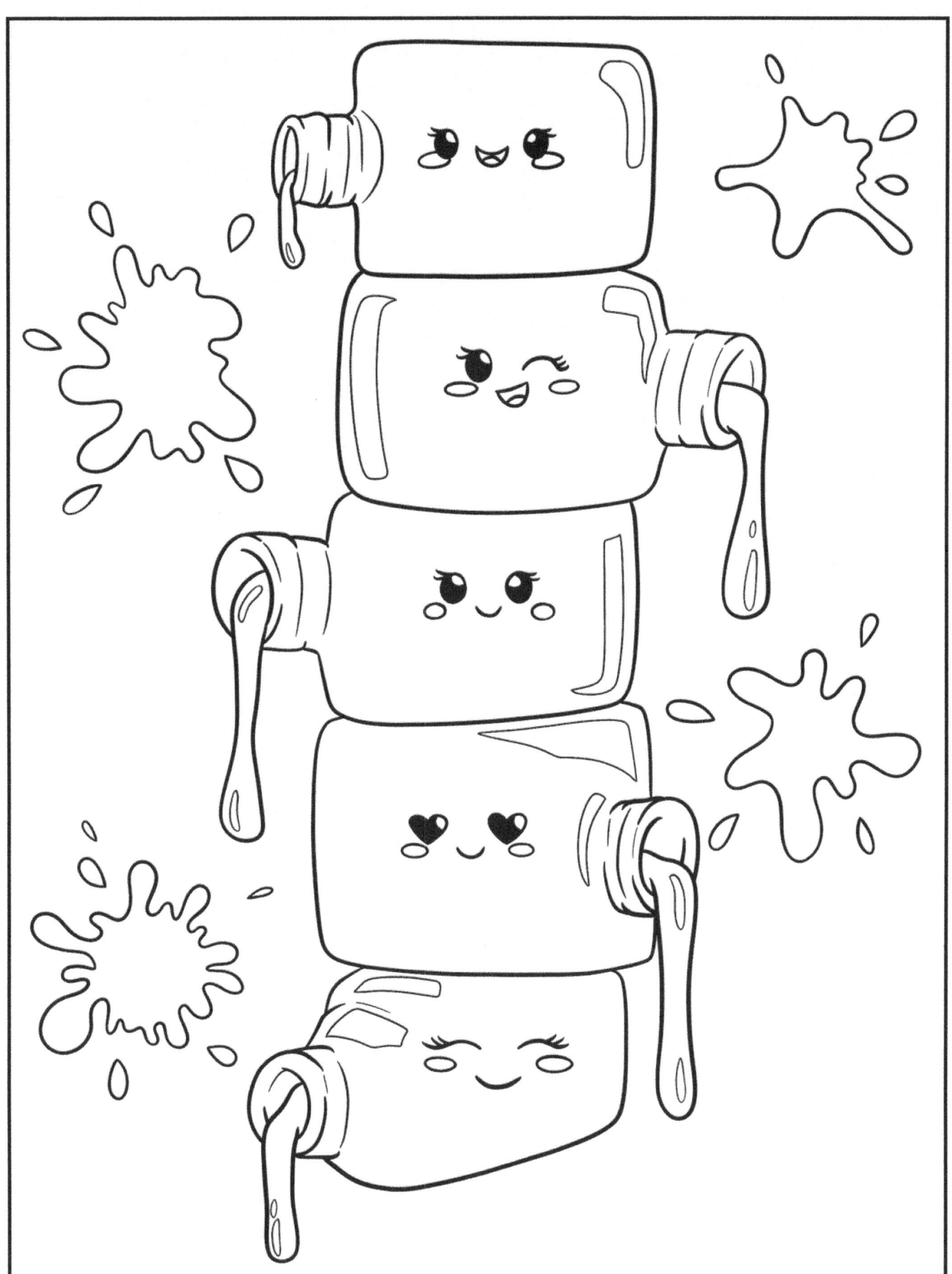

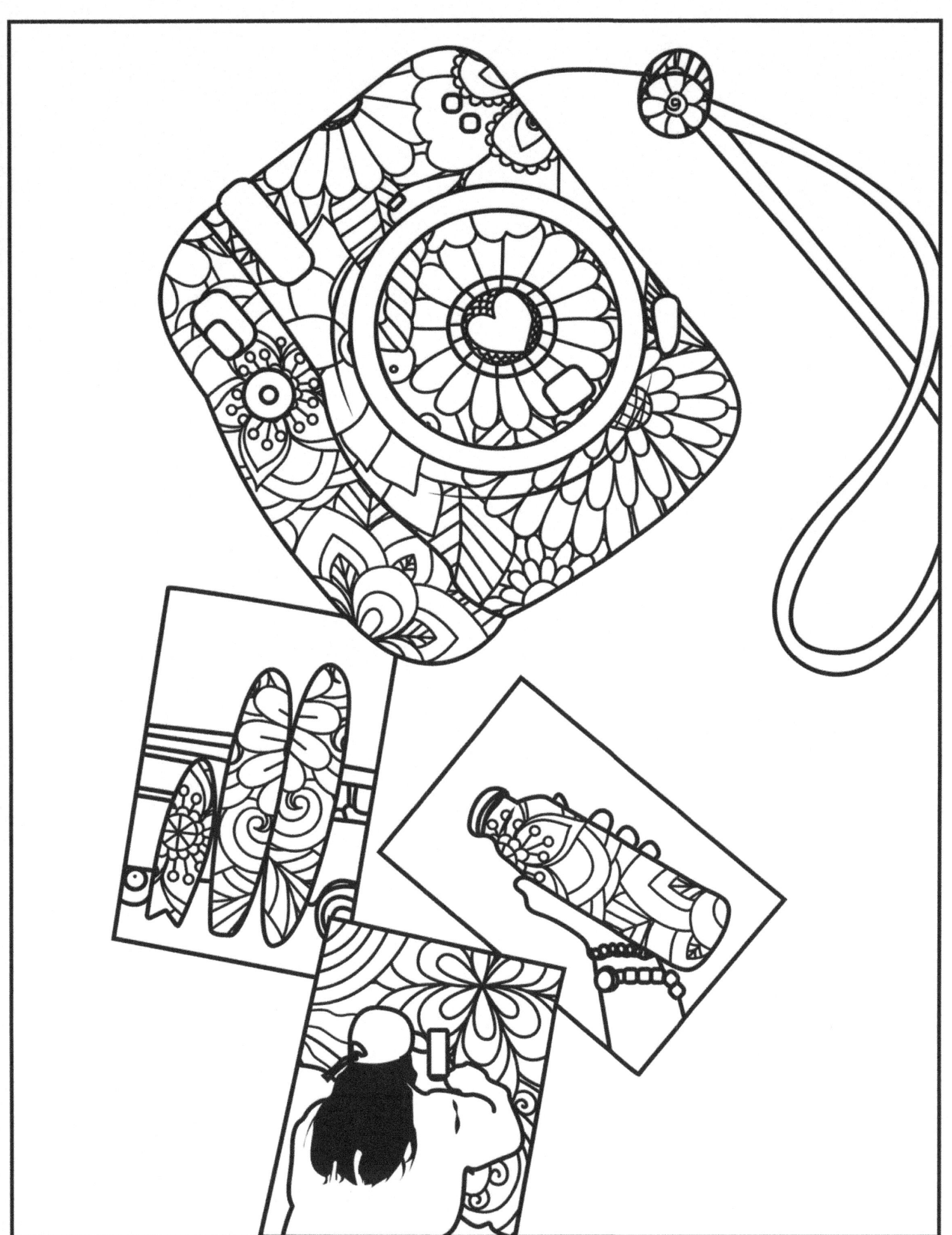

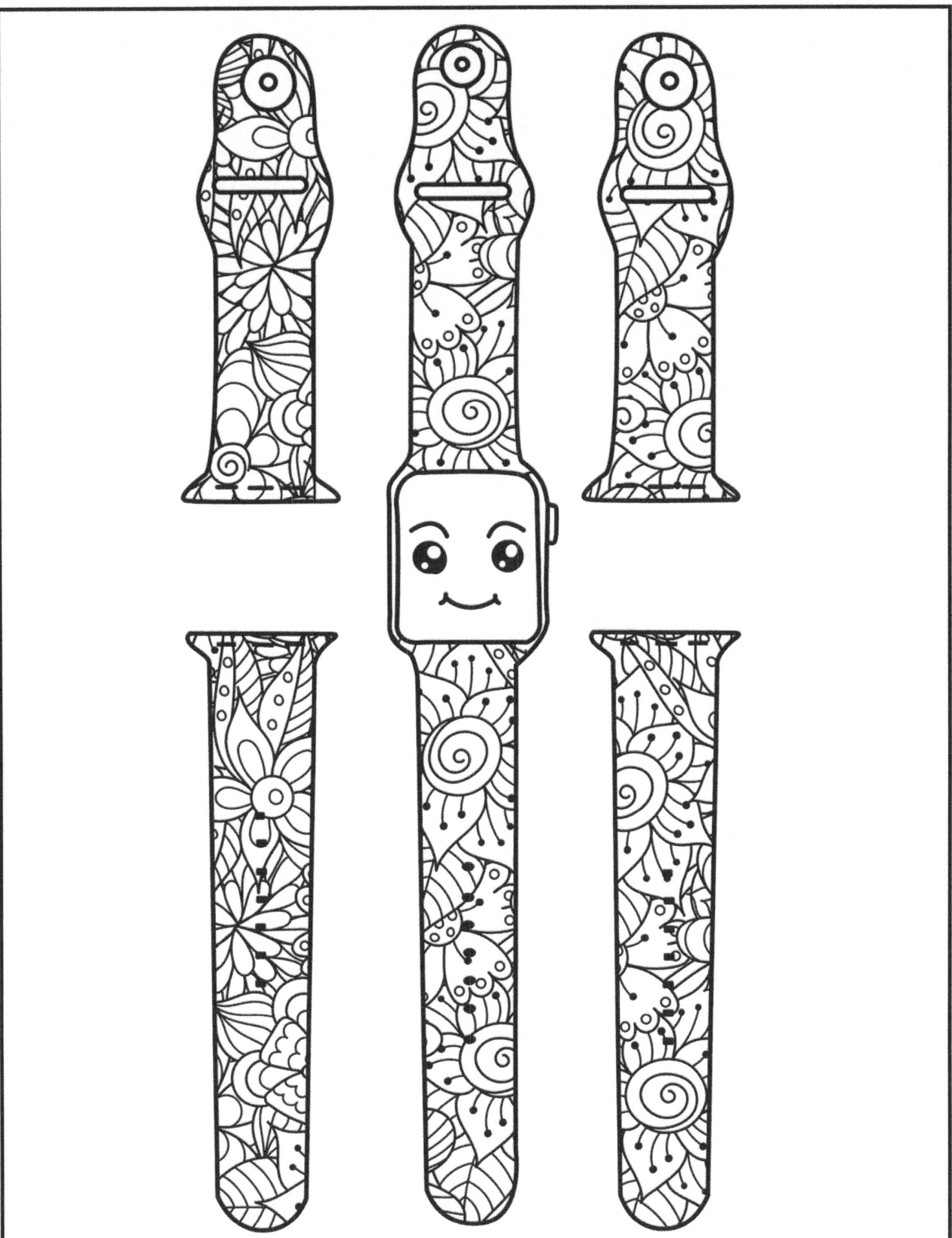

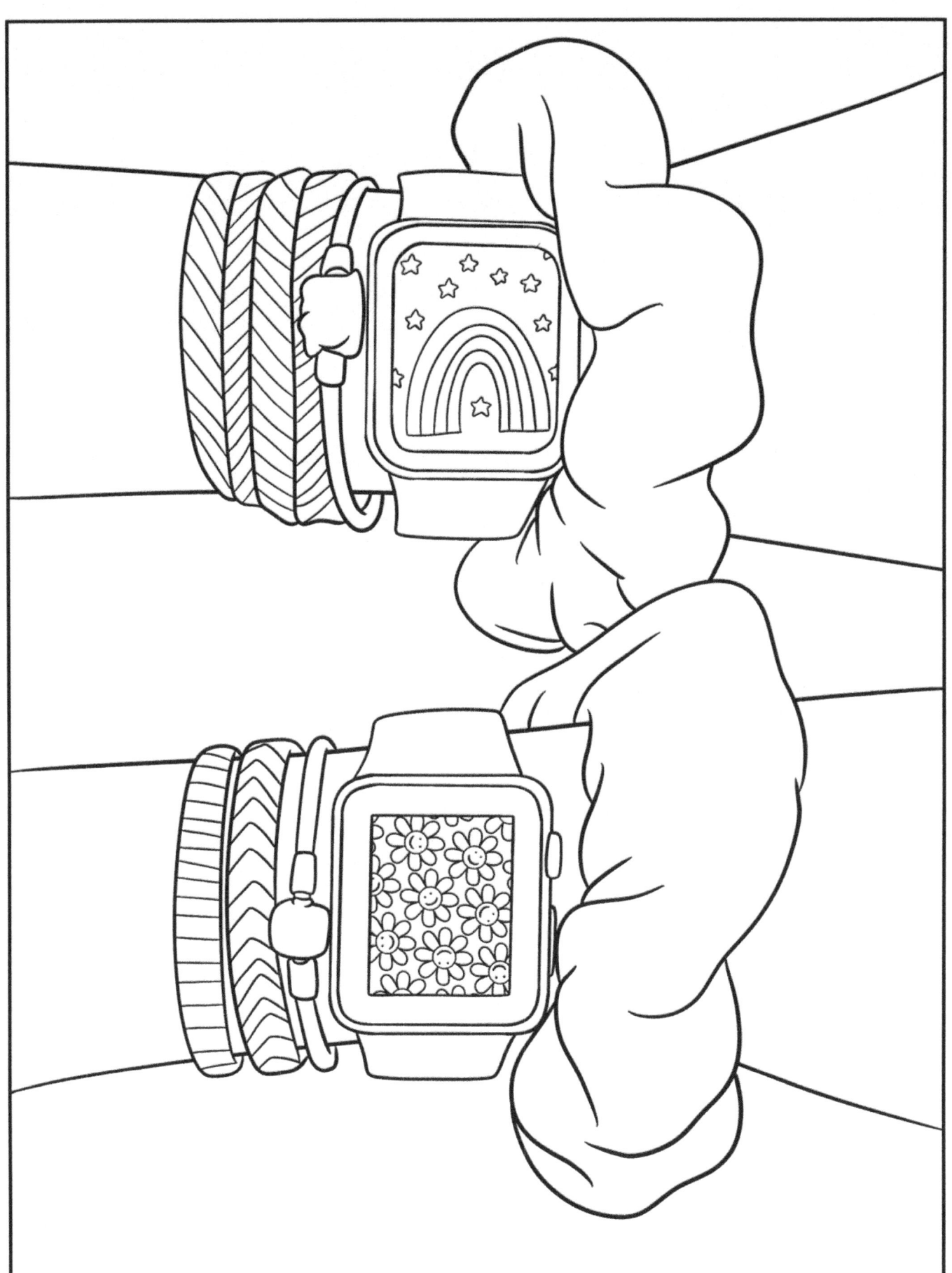

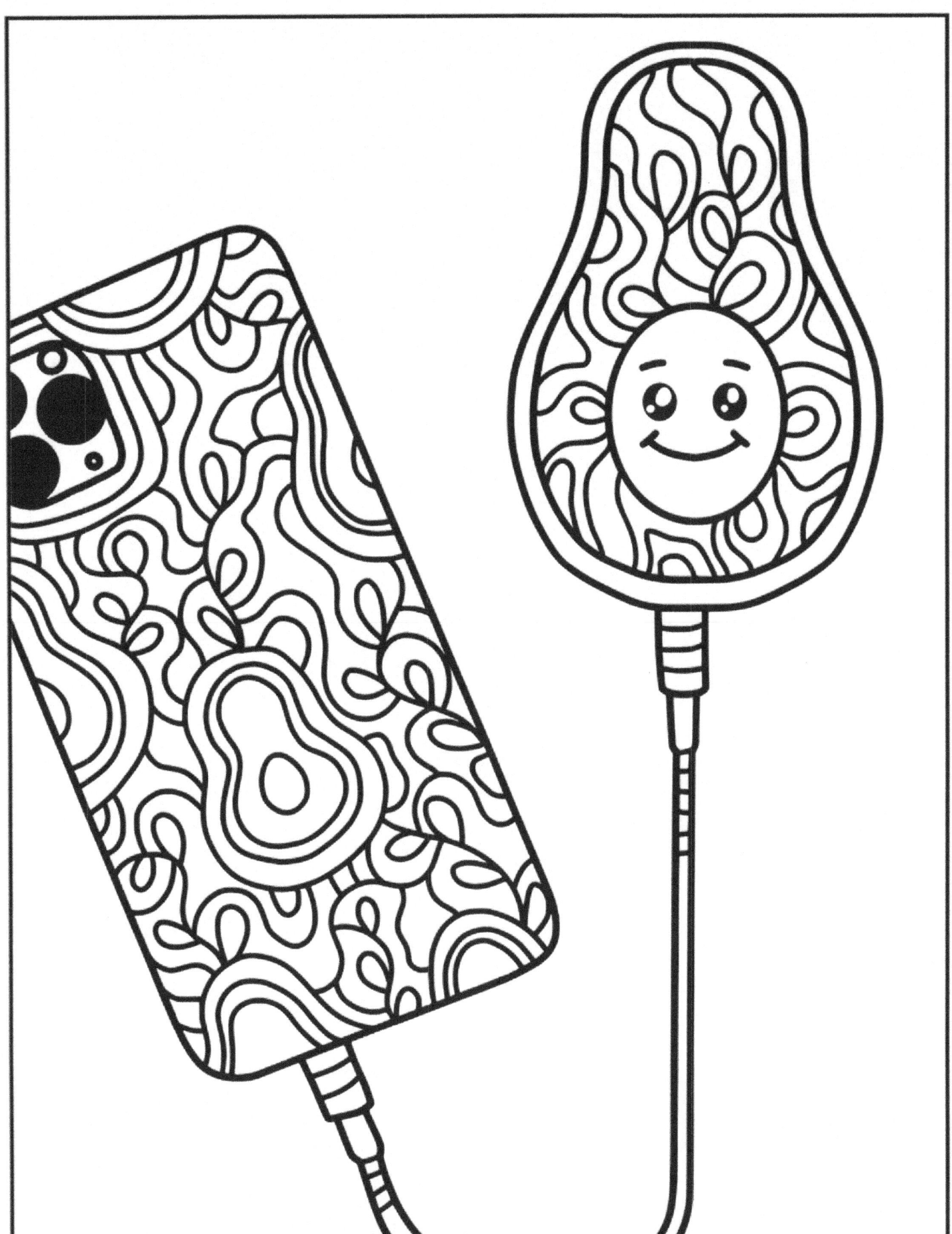

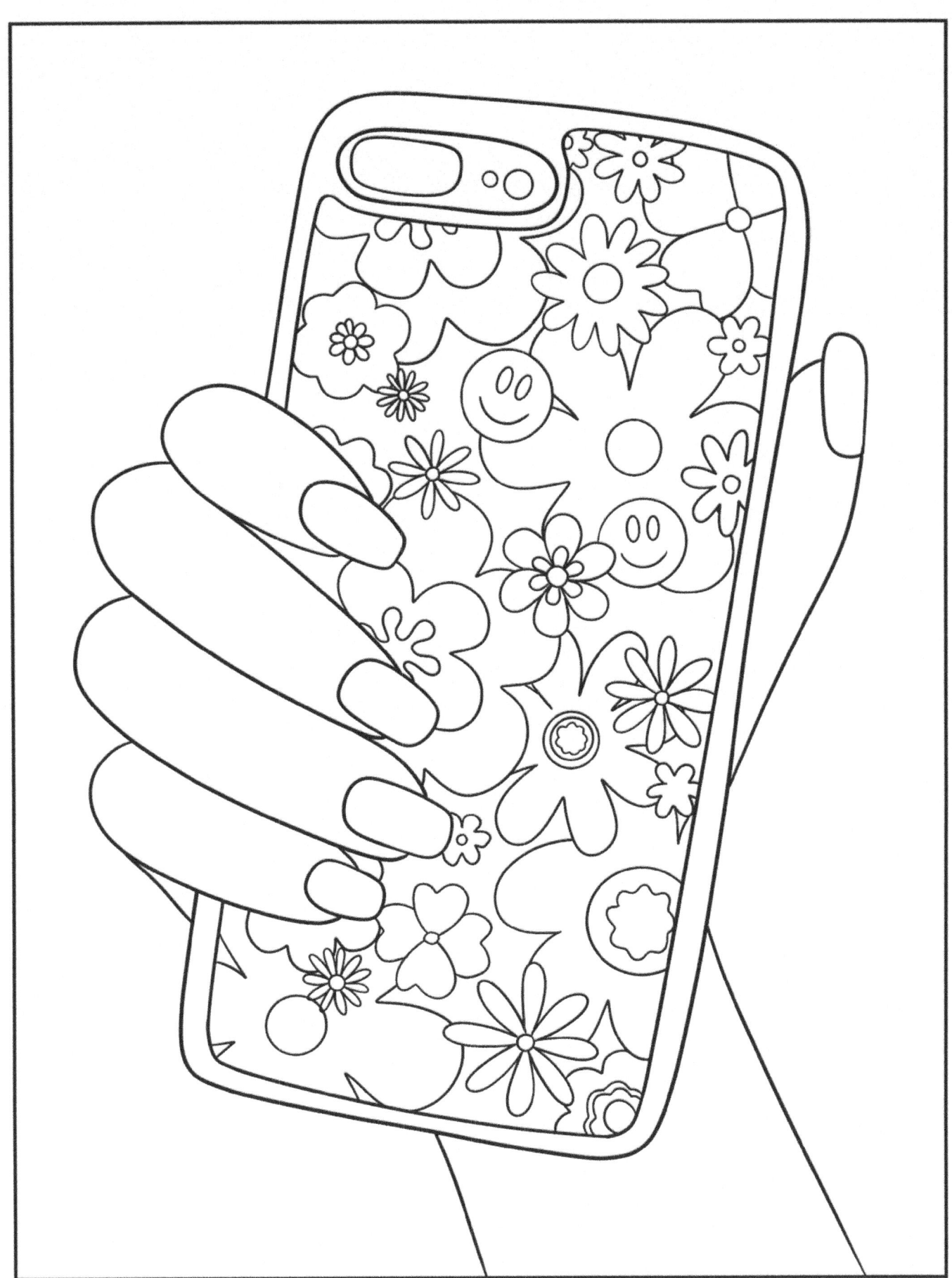

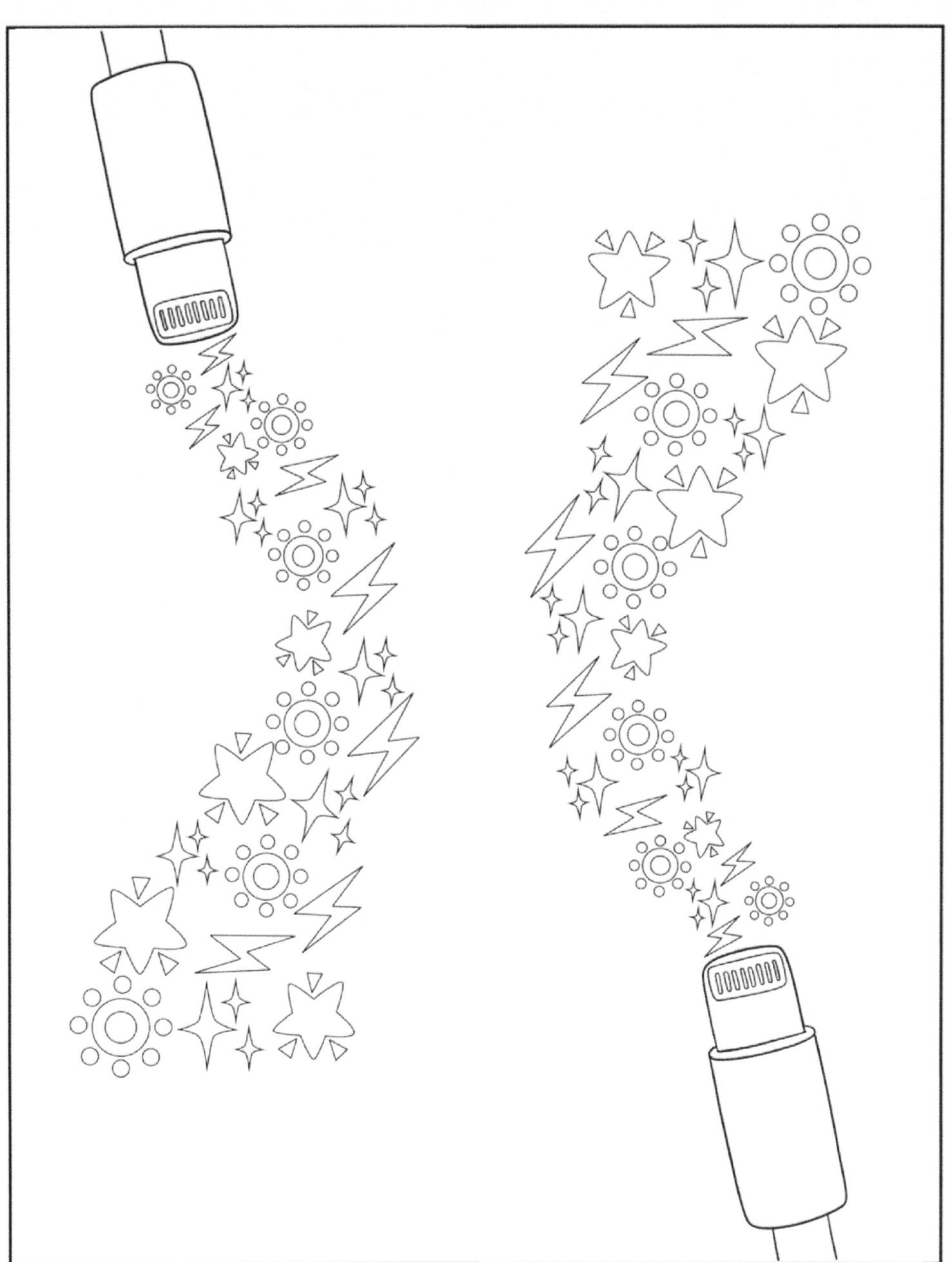

We hope you enjoyed the coloring book!

We would love you to leave a review on Amazon - it really helps other people who love coloring to find our books.

The easiest way to do this is to find the book on Amazon (Fun Animals Coloring Book), scroll to the customer review section and share your thoughts.

Thank you!

All available through Amazon:

Amazon.com
Amazon.co.uk
Amazon.ca
Amazon.com.au

Or visit the links on our website or Instagram Bio

www.ellastevensondesigns.com

@ellastevensondesigns

Fun Animals
Coloring book

40 Cool and Creative Animal Pictures for Tweens and Teens

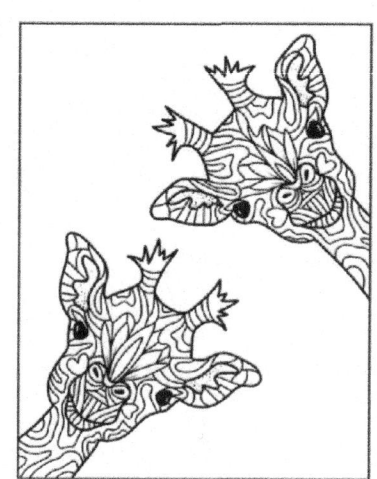

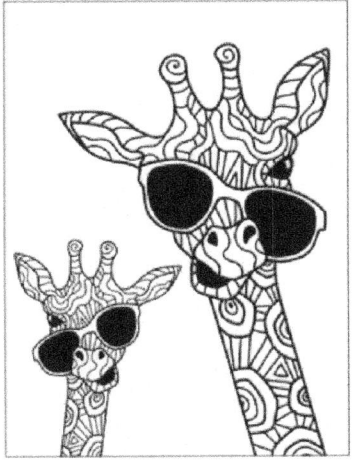

HORSE
COLORING BOOK FOR GIRLS

40 Creative and Original
Designs for Tweens and Teens

Made in the USA
Las Vegas, NV
13 April 2025

20885609R00052